THE *Vine* IS *Mine*

THE *Vine* IS *Mine*

The Unripe Grape

FRANCES IRENE

authorHOUSE

AuthorHouse™
1663 Liberty Drive
Bloomington, IN 47403
www.authorhouse.com
Phone: 1 (800) 839-8640

Published by AuthorHouse   11/21/2015

ISBN: 978-1-5049-2709-3 (sc)
ISBN: 978-1-5049-2710-9 (hc)
ISBN: 978-1-5049-2708-6 (e)

Library of Congress Control Number: 2015912488

Print information available on the last page.

All scripture quotations are from the King James Version.

CONTENTS

May 2015

Dear Readers:

As I prayed, I did not know what to say. God knew what I had been going through day after day. He knew what was on my mind and the daily desires of my broken heart! I knew that he would bring me through, in his own promised time.

While down on my back, I journeyed to and from (in and out), not knowing which way I must go. I was confident that this mishap should not happen to a lifetime Christian, or so I thought. I will never forget how my heart took leaps and bounds. My heart gave way to time; I was in a new dimension. Moses called it "Holy Ground."

Frances Irene is a dynamic woman of great faith, a seasoned Christian who struggled with her faith daily until one day a grape revealed the vision of her plot, plan, and purpose in life! Her heart and mind were under a command to "go back and complete the started plan"!

The Vine Is Mine is an incredible insight of searchable wisdom demonstrating the labor force of Christianity, our faith.

Frances Irene

Author

THE UNRIPE GRAPE

Seasoning is the flavoring of time. It is the time when character is developed, values are reclassified, and visions are imposed and exposed. There are three basic cultivating segments of the time frame of cycles: We are born. We live. We die (the physical death). There is no escape. These are the facts of life. No matter who we think we are, all of us have a birth date, the day God breathed into us the breath of life and we became a living soul full of "His image and likeness." All of us have a destiny date. When the final light goes out and the picture frame is empty, the privilege to survive is no longer ours to cherish; we fall asleep. Our season in this life is over.

Seasons are the in-between time of life and death. At best, life offers us happy times or sad times, weeping times or rejoicing times, painful times and growing times. None of these moments will last forever. Seasons come and seasons go. They are in complete harmony with time in transition, transaction, and transformation. However, they do bring forth their own accomplishments in God's appointed time. Time has a wavering control over the seasons, but God is indefinite. He controls both time and seasons, because God is always on time. Our journey in life is the reason for the season: "To everything there is a season, and a time to every purpose under the heaven" (Ecclesiastes 3:1).

My season, the call, is not as spectacular as the burning bush. I did not hear a voice from heaven saying, "take off your shoes, this is holy ground." I have had my share of problems, misplacement of character, unfair implementation, yet they have not been as dramatic as Jacob's ladder. I saw no extended ladder or angels ascending to and descending from heaven. I am not like Abram; God has not instructed me to leave my home to search for a promised land. From age six, I have always heard a voice from within telling me, "Yes, go ahead it is yours." And there has been an assurance that everything is going to be all right. Many times my struggles have been unbearable—so intensified it seemed as if God's voice was silent. Other times the voice has said, "Wait." This has resulted in the most difficult of times, but also the most rewarding experiences of my life. It was during these difficult moments that my spirit has awakened to what God is speaking, and He says, "Hold on a little while longer." Out of the flames comes pure gold. Out of struggle comes a stronger faith. Each time God brings me through, I want to exalt Him and give Him more praise, power, and glory.

Is my calling sure? My strongest desire in life is to win souls for Jesus Christ, especially those of babies and young people. I have been through many trials, temptations, and snares. I have been confused to the point that I did not know myself, and believe me, I was not crazy either. I have been blinded with discouragement, knocked down with disappointment, trampled over with despair.

My family and close friends were not aware of my drama; they never even suspected my experiences. I had fallen, and I could not move. This spiritual warfare I could not share. It was a wilderness experience I had to go through. What do you do when life becomes intensified and unbearable and God's voice seems silent? Hold on just a little longer—God is at work. Pray continuously that your heart fails Him not.

Why the heart, Lord? It is the center of traumatic emotions. Within the heart is the realization and revelation of the true self. The heart agitates, filters, and eliminates wrong thinking for rightful living. The heart commands and demands our actions and reactions to be drawn to obedience. Question: Lord, when will you come to me? Answer: When you behave yourself wisely! When you talk and walk in your house (your body) in my word with a heart that seeks to do my perfect will every day.

My calling is simple: I have a strong desire to love God and Jesus Christ and to do His holy will. My earnest fervent prayer is, "Lord, tell me your will for my life. Give me the courage and strength to do your perfect will."

From the time I was six years old until now is a span of a lifetime. The season is about to change. Now I can tell the world that God is real, and Jesus Christ is my Lord and Savior without a doubt! Lord, I am your open vessel! Lord, sanctify me so that I can glorify you! A calling is not seasonal; therefore, one has to be seasoned for the calling. Here I am, Lord, season me for your glory! "Ye are my witnesses, saith the Lord, and my servant whom I have chosen: that ye may know and believe me, and understand that I am he: before me there was no God formed, neither shall there be after me" (Isaiah 43:10).

GETTING TO KNOW GOD

Belief is the absolute acceptance of that which exists—the very essence of admitting that those things imagined are real. It is the innate ability to agree according to one's free will. Belief is taken for granted. It yields to face value. It is based on the acceptance of one's word without doubt, fear, question, or compromise. I believe that God created the heavens and the earth. I was not an eyewitness of the dramatic forces of God's Holy Spirit in dynamic actions as He moved to create His marvelous works. I have read about it in the Bible. I accept it as the foundation of my being. I believe everything God said in His word. The acceptance of the creation is the basis for all truths: "In the beginning, God created the heaven and the earth" (Genesis 1:1).

I believe God *was*, because I believe God *is*. I believe God still *is*, because I *am*! Life in its simplest form points to His greatness. My existence is evidence of a greater existence. He is still the great "I Am"!

Belief is an unwavering experience out of touch with reality, and yet it is as real as reasoning. It goes beyond self-indulgence and eyewitness: I don't know, I don't need to know, there is no need to persuade. As long as I have a choice, I choose to believe in God.

The perceptions of believing are incredible. The innocent belief displays come from the power within us. There is an unlimited source of strength and joyful surprises when you believe in God's wonderful word. The unknown is exciting, as new, immeasurable mercies unfold moment by moment. What is so very incredible about belief is the dynamics of its rewards. Believing is stress free and brings satisfaction without effort. Believe "With God all things are possible" (Matthew 19:26) and *it shall be*.

Belief is powerful! It comes from the heart, not the mind. From the surface it seems weak, because it can be blocked. Once belief pierces the heart, it gains strength to encourage. The greatest extension of belief is the ability to develop courage. When others see a strong belief in God, it is overpowering. It will reverse any hopeless situation, and it will start an avalanche of potential events. The impossible becomes possible, hopeless changes to hopeful, and the negative is exchanged for the positive. Belief imparts power when it tells the mind what the heart needs to know, because it signifies that everything is going to be all right.

We cannot remain in one level of belief for a lifetime. We cannot stay there, because life is a continuous process. As much as belief is a comfortable zone, we must grow from one stage to another. Steadfast belief teaches us how to grow without fear, doubt, or anxiety, and it advances us to a higher level.

I believe God was, because I believe God is.

I believe God still is, *because I* am!

He is still the great "I Am"!

Faith gains conviction and victory. It is upon the confession

of faith that we live daily. We never know what trials will

demonstrate our extended faith. Only through faith can we

come forth as pure as gold. Our beliefs will not do it; neither will our trust. Why not? Because each is dependent upon the other. Faith means that I, and I alone, am standing on the promises of God. Faith is where belief and trust merge to fulfill the hope of glory in Jesus Christ.

So very often, I have heard and have said, "All I had to depend on was Jesus! Jesus was all I had left!" What a terrible misconception to put limitations on God. If we think about it, Jesus is the total sum of all we will ever need. He is the source of all of our strength. He is the fourth man in the fiery furnace. He is the foundation of faith. He has never been a last-minute expectation. He has always been in the mix. He has always been on time and in time. Thank you, Lord, you never left me alone in the midnight crises of life. You promised that you would never leave me alone. Thank you, Jesus. You have kept your promise. Faith has taught me that you always keep your promises … for you told me in your word and a dream that, "Lo, I am with you always, even until the end of the world" (Matthew 28:20). Thank you, precious savior. You did not let me go.

Faith is the step-up process of expectations, the most sensitive dimension in life and its outcome. Without faith, life becomes tired and weary. With faith, life is more energized by our memory of prior knowledge and innate ability of what God can do and what God will do! Is there anything too hard for God? With faith, life can be approached in a more practical way. There is nothing too hard for God! New beginnings open doors to the world where greater expectations of life can be fulfilled by God.

Faith is the step-up process of expectations,

the most sensitive dimension in life and its outcome!

THIRST

Thirst is the craving for water. When you crave water, nothing else will do. Nothing will satisfy your thirst like a cool drink of water. We need natural water to survive. Natural water satisfies the body, but it cannot fill up the soul.

In the beginning, God blew into man the breath of life, and man became a living soul with a spiritual birth. The natural water flows into the supernatural and overflows the soul. Jesus is the supernatural water. He fills the void to its capacity and opens the floodgates with an abundant life.

Look at the woman at the well. She was naturally thirsty for the supernatural water, but she did not know it. She was also an empty vessel, but she did not know it. She had heard of Jesus, but did not know Him. Her plan was normal. She planned to fill her pot with natural water and go back home to the same messed-up lifestyle. But the day she met Jesus, her life changed drastically. Her thirst was over! She had to drop whatever was holding her back! She had to run! She had to shout! She had to tell others! The supernatural water compels the overflow; it causes a flood to burst loose in your spirit. You cannot keep it to yourself!

Have you ever experienced a time in your life when everything you touched became brittle and crumbled? You searched and searched for someone or something, and you reached out, and nothing was there. Let's face it. You were in a drought! Nothing was going to satisfy you except the supernatural water. When you drink the supernatural water from Jesus, the thirst is over! This is where I was when I slipped and fell.

The slip came before the fall. When you are confronted with a slip, you lose your balance, and you are totally out of control. The situation is not only helpless; it is hopeless.

We all have slipped at one time or another.

A slip comes before the fall.

The barriers are broken; desire diminishes; strength converts into shock; and before you know it, you are in a state of nothing. These chains of events happened to me without a trace of my awareness. Had I known the danger—if only I could have seen it coming—I would have done everything in my power to prevent this tragic mishap. Once in a slip, there is no way out, not even a chance for change. There is no turning back. The slip will not let you go! You must go with the flow. You are in your season!

We have all slipped at one time or another. Slipping is easy. We have been cautioned: "Watch out for that banana peel." "Don't step on a wet or greasy floor." Some of us have been warned about slippery, tricky relationships. We have been told the best way to maintain a habit is not to slip back into it. If I eat one potato chip, you better believe a whole bag will be gone in no time flat. The cause is easy, but the effects of its consequences are complicated. Here I was, flat on the floor, looking upward as I heard someone calling to me, "Don't move! Don't move! You have slipped on a grape!"

I cannot tell you why things happened to me on that Sunday afternoon without sharing the before and after events. Two hours before my fall, I was safe in my mother-in-law's house taking Holy Communion. She was homebound. The outreach ministry of the church had appointed two deacons to administer Holy Communion to the sick and shut-ins. The worship was beautiful! The deacons served the bread (Jesus Christ's Body) and the wine (Jesus Christ's Blood) with a prayer of thanksgiving. After the Holy Meal, we sang a hymn. It was an exquisite, delightful worship.

I should not have gone shopping on a Sunday. I should have remembered the Fourth Commandment: "Remember the sabbath day, to keep it holy" (Exodus 20:8). As a Sunday school teacher for forty years, I should not only have known it, I should have lived it. I was determined to cook my mother-in-law a home-cooked meal, because all she had been eating were take-out meals. After all, wasn't that the reason for my 420-mile trip? Wasn't that my mission? Guilty. I needed God's mercy and forgiveness.

My mother-in-law, whom I affectionately call Mom, had been glad to see me. She told me to scrape up whatever was in the refrigerator, but I was determined to cook her a home-cooked meal. She also told me not to go to the store. I should have remembered that God is a Holy God, twenty-four/seven, and his words are everlasting truths that travel within us wherever we go. Instead of listening to her God-given wisdom, I left the house in a cab only to find myself in the grocery store, flat on my back on the floor.

Inadvertently, I had slipped into something. I could not get out without change. One moment I was walking upright headed in the right direction, but apparently I went the wrong way. Countless times I have asked myself why. Without a warning, I slipped on something as insignificant as a grape, which stopped me and changed my whole life.

A fall can be dangerous to the body, mind, and soul. The slip determines the extent of the fall. When you slip, you spin into a state of numbness. You could keep on slipping, if your body does not give way to a stronger source. Sin works that way, too. Through disobedience, Adam and Eve slipped into sin. One day they had fellowship with God, and within countless time, they slipped into something they could not get out of.

It is a fact the slip comes before the fall. A slip can take you into a place you do not want to be. The dilemma entraps the situation and it is over- powering. You have fallen and you can't move. The painful truth is that you keep on falling deeper and deeper, if there is no exchange to hold you up. Our daily prayer should always be, "And lead us not into temptation, but deliver us from evil" (Matthew 6:13).

A slip has a strong hold; it pulls you down to the bottom. You can't go any further, because you have already arrived. It is the crushing point of the designation. The word *if* becomes an extension of blame: if I had (had not) done this, that would not have happened. The crushing point is where accountability tells you that perhaps you might or might not have been responsible for past experiences. The breaking point is the realization that it is your life, and it is your turn to be responsible for the outcome of future situations. Get over it and strive higher for bigger and better things in Jesus's name. You cannot do it alone.

Accessibility clearly states: whatever the fall, you cannot stay in this boundless condition. You must rise! The question is, how does one rise when one is lying in a pool of numbness (sin)? The outcome of the rise depends greatly on the acceptance of the fall. A slip has one aim, and that is to land you anywhere you fall. It determines the extent of the fall. How you rise depends greatly on your outlook of the inner self—your faith in God.

God is a Holy God. You must come to Him confessing from the heart. Word of mouth cannot always be trusted. When you are crushed, shattered, almost destroyed, the heart feels the piercing, unforgettable pain. Confession is where the slip meets the fall. Words from the heart cry out, "Lord, forgive me."

Secondly, the slip encounters a head-on collision with truth. God is a righteous and merciful God. He even gives sinners rights. If you are in a sinful stage of life, don't forget your rights. You have the right to believe and confess as well as to expect and accept forgiveness. You have the right to reject these rights, because God gave you the right of free will. Remember, God has the final right to grant salvation. To request a place in His Kingdom, you must cry out the name of Jesus! Jesus Christ will hear your cry and redeem you from all your sins. Lord, forgive me! Lord, save me! It is done!

Fall in love with God. His power is matchless. He is our God of a second chance. Get right with Him and stay right with Him. He gives sinners the right to repent and be saved in Jesus's name. "For thou art great, and doest wondrous things: thou art God alone." (Psalm 86:10)

A slip is geared toward a downward bounce because our natural position is an upward trend. Advancement concludes that only a loving, caring, powerful God can lift you out of this mess. It is then you realize you can't stay in that fallen position. "With God all things are possible" (Matthew 19:26). Rise up in the name of Jesus!

While lying on the floor, I looked at the crumbled-up grape. It was so cold, so still, so broken, lying at my feet. Grapes are my favorite fruit, but that grape was not the object of my affection at that moment. How could something so small cause me so much pain and suffering? Don't be deceived by its size. The strength was in the substance, not the size. It was not until the inside came out that the power was released and the damage was done. We must be ever so careful not to let our thoughts, actions, and behavior control us inwardly until our imaginations become massive elements of self-destruction.

My Grandmother Ida used to sing, "Keep the devil running and the world can't do you no harm." Pray the devil out! Sing him out! Shout him out! Keep him out anyway you can. Know that the struggle is yours, but the battle is God's. He will divide and defeat. Humble yourself to God's submission. Reach up and reach out. Jesus will meet you in the pathway of your fall, and Jesus will raise you up unto Him. Amen!

The dynamic of an affliction can be a blessing in disguise, guiding you to a place where you need to be. Along with the fall, or shortly thereafter, you will go into a valley of pain and suffering. My physical fall took me into deep pain, but a higher spiritual sphere—a place in faith

I had never experienced before. Pain, suffering, and faith are locked down, intertwined, and bounded by the intensity of our personal beliefs and experiences. Out of pain and suffering comes a stronger faith in Jesus Christ, the hope of glory. Pain and suffering come, and pain and suffering go. God always provides an escape! No pain, no gain! Pain and suffering will either increase or decrease your faith. No wavering! No compromising! No modifying! Jesus said, "Have faith in God" (Mark 11:22).

Four months later, I was hospitalized due to the slip and fall. In the emergency room, my pain scored a ten and beyond on a scale of one to ten. My heart skipped frantic beats. It roared like my 1967 Impala when it needed a jump-start. What do you do when you think it is your time to let go? Are you really ready? Truthfully, I was not! I was not afraid to go back from where I had come, but I was afraid that my soul would be lost. Envision this: everything in heaven is holy. God is our Holy Father. Jesus Christ is His Holy Son. The Angels are all holy. Here on earth, I was guilty of breaking the Fourth Commandment: "Remember the sabbath day, to keep it holy" (Exodus 20:8).

I believe that we will be changed in the twinkling of the eye. I know how to pray. I know how to praise God. The most vital requirement of faith is to obey God's words and live to please Him daily. Release the vision. The verdict is guilty! "God, please forgive me. Father, I have sinned against you!"

Whom do you call when you are already in the emergency room and your heart needs a jump-start? I called to the nearest doctor. She responded, "You are not my patient." The nurses were extremely busy. Here I was, once again, on my back. I dared not move, but I was lying in a good position.

The position you fall in is vital to the way you get up. When you fall, you will be face up or face down. Neither is a good position. Falling is serious and can be life threatening. However, when you fall face down, it is less complicated.

If you can move your limbs, you can get up with little or no difficulty.

If you end up lying down with your face up and your back against the surface, you have fallen on fallow ground. This can be a crippling position that can leave you embarrassed, confused, and hurt. But face up was a better position for me. Although I could not get up, I was looking up! What a good place to be!

As I lay on the stretcher, my spirit came alive and commanded that I call on the name above all names: Jesus! He is never too busy. Call Jesus. I quickly obeyed that familiar voice from within. I started calling, not in a loud voice, but I cried deep down in my soul: *Jesus! Jesus! Jesus!*

Before I knew it, a host of nurses were ripping off my clothes. I felt the intravenous needle go into my arm. Electrocardiogram wires were all over me. I felt my heart as it flipped, fluttered, and flopped. Thank you, Jesus! You interceded, and God did not allow it to stop. Jesus, Jesus, Jesus! Everything you need is in the name of Jesus!

A sonogram revealed a dangerous blood clot in my left leg. Praise your holy name, dear Jesus. You kept me here for a reason. Lord, here am I. Send me.

Whatever position you fall into—spiritual denial, family opposition, generational curses, health crises, temptations (big or small), financial hardships, slippery and tricky relationships—remember that life at its best will inflict pain and suffering many times to accomplish God's purpose in your life. Faith activated will pursue faith in action. Do not be moved! Take hold of your position. You were designed to stand. While lying face up, take advantage of the upright position. Consider your ways as clearer images come into view. Your past focuses beyond the possibilities of the present as you grip *faith* for the potentials of the future. (If only you would get up.)

When you have fallen, realize that you have hit rock bottom. Why not wait on the Lord? While you are waiting, have a 'Jesus praise party' all by yourself. Make a clown out of the devil. Wait for Jesus to show up! There is joy—unspeakable joy—in the presence of the Lord! Although I was in tremendous pain, it fascinated me to see that the Lord is good! "His mercy endureth forever" (Psalm 136:1).

The completion of any fall is to get back up. When you fall, don't give up, and don't give in. Get back up, and don't fall again. If you do, without forgiveness you are doomed. Be confident and know that prayer denied is another prayer in process. Hold on! Don't let go! God knows what is best for your life! This is only a test.

Although a slip and a fall are closely related, there is a vast difference between them. A slip separates circumstances, reasoning, and conditions. It will disconnect anything in its downward pathway. It will go deeper and deeper with an intractable force. The painful truth is that life's trenches have the same effect. The cutting edge goes deep. When you slip, you are already in the gap. This is the way out: open your heart, lift high your voice, and shout, "I love you,

God! I love you, Jesus! I know you love me! Thank you, Lord, for everything, in Jesus's name! Amen!

A fall connects the impact, blocks continuation, and influences change. It transcends circumstances, transfers reasoning, and transforms conditions. Once you have fallen, you will never be the same when you get back up again. We must realize that God has not completed His creation until He has *saved all*. He wants us to go as far as our faith in Him takes us, and He will complete the work He started in all of us.

Nothing's Wrong with a Struggle

There is nothing wrong with a struggle.

As long as you know what you are

Struggling for and to whom the praise,

Honor, and glory belongs.

There is nothing wrong with a struggle.

Pain gains victory and crushes defeat.

Good times, bad times, sad times

Life tastes the bitter with the sweet.

There is nothing wrong with a struggle.

Strength is regained, good character

Is maintained. Humbleness in pride is

Sustained.

There is nothing wrong with a struggle.

Faith

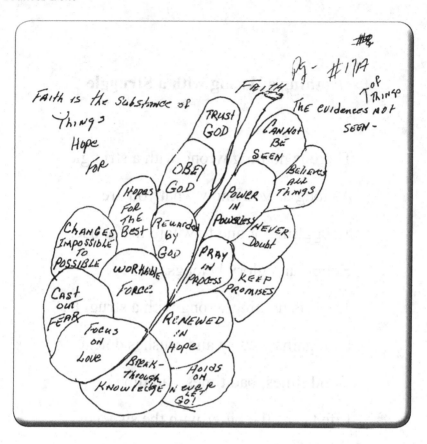

Faith is the substance of

Things

Hoped

For ...

The evidences of things not seen.(Hebrew 11:1)

FOOTPRINTS OF FORGIVENESS

Life gives us many malfunctions, misconceptions, and plenty of misjudgments. It is easy to make a mistake! We walk into situations by omission or commission. Many times we become our worst enemy due to our circumstances. We become disconnected when we fail to recognize and accept God's goodness. We are deceived because we do not believe in God's almighty power to forgive. The Golden Rule tells us: Do unto others as you will have them do unto you. This is something we do not hear about in today's world; rather, our universal concept and practice seems to be: Do unto others before they do unto us. In all situations, I have learned from the challenges of life to focus on the "goodness" of God rather than to give in to the forces of evil. These mishaps have made me stronger, because they have taught me to rise, soar, and shine.

To hold a grudge against anyone puts life in a vulnerable position. You are holding all of the resentment, animosity, and hurt and the person or persons responsible are either unaware of their cause and effect or they couldn't really care less about you or the situation. Yes, it did hurt during the time it happened and afterwards. It will continue to hurt if you do not compromise. Forgiveness is the compromise between good and evil (right or wrong). It is the obligation to submit and surrender. It is the gap between release and relief. It happened! It is over! Nothing was done in the past! Nothing can be done about it now! God is the final judge.

Jesus was the perfect sacrifice! He cried out from the cross, "Father, forgive them; for they know not what they do" (Luke 23:34). Forgiveness is Jesus' divine purpose. "My God, my God, why hast thou forsaken me?" (Matthew 27:46). God, who is righteous, could not accept sin. In The Garden of Eden, man was the apple of God's eye. When Jesus cried out, he was bearing our sins. On the cross, reconciliation was restored through the blood sacrifice to forgive our sin.

Forgiveness is the ultimate nature of God.

Love embraces it!

Faith exhibits it!

Redemption enhances it!

Salvation ensures it!

The prayer of forgiveness

Is always answered.

Forgiveness is the ultimate nature of God! God's plan for man is based on forgiveness. Throughout the Holy Scripture, the foundational theme is "forgiveness." Love embraces it. Faith exhibits it. Redemption enhances it. Salvation ensures it. The prayer of forgiveness is always answered.

I began to visualize my recovery time as a wilderness journey. In the domain of the wild—land totally isolated, desolate, uncultivated, and uninhabited—fearsome beasts roam around cunningly attracting, skillfully tracking, and masterfully attacking their prey. Evildoers are constantly lurking around in the pathway of life seeking those they can jerk out of the will of God.

The wilderness is a place of survival. It is also a place of conditioning where we can be positioned for our purpose in Jesus Christ. It is a no-man's-land, but God is there. The passageway is narrow, and the distance is blurred as you stumble aimlessly walking in circles. You can see, but you are deceived and restrained by the visions as you try to go through. Entrapped, you question life because you were born to live and not die!

The appearance of belief visualizes and discloses the reality of the invisible forces before the eyes. The right to passage cannot be seen with the naked eye. Sight becomes insight as the light gives away to darkness. The untamed imagination runs wild. You search for what you hope to find among the vanished and lost. Clearly you wander and ponder here, there, and everywhere, seeking a way out of this barren land. Without God's purpose there is no destiny. Whenever destiny is lost, you are already in a wilderness.

When you are lost in the wilderness, confusion invades all aspects of life. It works behind every scene cluttering and casting diversions of anxiety and fear. Ingratitude, unforgiveness, revenge, jealousy, and envy rage from a stony heart. Hesitation is suspended in the thickened haze of a weakened will. Perplexity no longer knows what to make of the circumstances. Determination trembles as uncontrollable thoughts block the blessings that God has already prepared for us. Uncertainty and doubt run wild as deception viciously roams throughout the mind. It is an unpurified life that has violated God's will. We must become purified to live forever with Him. The questions come to mind, Will I ever get well? Will I ever be able to go to church again to worship in the sanctuary?

Jesus was led into the wilderness, not because he had sinned. He was led into the wilderness because He knew that the burdens of life would drive us there one day. He provided a way out! When tempted by the devil, Jesus accessed the three-word password code: It is written! Jesus, working through the Holy Spirit, is the only way out. You are led into the wilderness by incapable will, depression, stress, frustration, sex—anything that you are not capable of overcoming. Struggles will entrap you and entangle the will to pursue it. These inconsistencies of emptiness and desperation can chase us into a wilderness journey. Whenever you spend more time wishing and thinking, rather than seeking, thanking, praising, praying, believing, and trusting, you will be lost in the wiles of life.

These wiles expand into a wasteland of barren moments of perilous time. Yet, we are positioned in this isolated place for two specific reasons. In the wilderness, we are chastened to be conformed into God's likeness by the renewal of our minds. It is a place of calling where we realize that self can no longer be measured by self. This place of experience is where God reveals His purpose for our lives.

The reflection of His image causes us to become a seeker after God's likeness. Likeness is absolute. Its appearance is a double congeneric parallel comparison to its connection. We are made in God's image; the fruit of the spirit reveals this. But we must be transformed into His likeness. There is no separation. The unity of oneness dominates the core from which we come. We are designed with a pattern of His approval, because we are sealed with God's goodness and chastened by His love.

Life within itself is a dynamic, ongoing, ever-increasing, one-time process commanded by God from the beginning.

The pivotal forces take us through many deviations and variations. From seedtime to harvest, buds to blossoms, fruitless to fruitful, unripened to ripened, birth to reproduction, we are transformed. Transformation is a miracle of performance that develops us from the original design—the "image" of God, our first birth—to the original intent, which transforms us into His "likeness," our second birth. According to our purpose, we change into our true identity, and we become Christlike. Jesus Christ is the vine; we are the fruit of the vine. The uniqueness of fruit is that it does not lose its true identity. Whether it grows in the wilderness or is cultivated on land, the natural process of an apple seed is to grow into an apple tree. Image reveals relationship, embraces acceptance, and predicts lineage of the heritage. Likeness, on the other hand, goes much deeper.

Likeness demands and commands an encounter with God. To gain power, a war must be fought, a victory must be declared, and a battle must be won. An encounter is not an exchange. An encounter is an absorption. It is an on-time experience when the Lord lays His hands on you! You are called out of darkness into the marvelous light. You must confront God for yourself. Ezekiel had a dry bones encounter. Paul was blinded on the Damascus Road. John's encounter was so deep it revealed what was to come, how it was coming, and what the future would be for the believers.

The Awakening—our encounter—will be the realization that God is the great "I Am." We will know him face to face. There will be nowhere to run! There will be nowhere to hide! One on one, face to face, up close and personal, we must repent! Repentance is the most overlooked part of salvation. Jesus has overpowered sin and conquered it all. Therefore, we must confront it in our lives to be reconciled back to God. In life, innocence collides with guilt. Guilt comes up against and tries to overturn good will and good intentions. Consciousness gives in to humility. Without the will of humility, there is no remission of sin. "Envy thou not the oppressor, and choose none of his ways" (Proverbs 3:31).

The will to be "like" God is manifested through the formation of humility. Humility floats into trust and obedience. Trust and obedience clash with fear and doubt. Faith and love bring us out! The resemblance of His likeness is in the absorption of our change. The more you encounter and endure God's will, the closer you get to being like God. Not God, but *like* Him. The resemblance of His likeness is in the absorption process of our encounter(s) with Him. An encounter can be a process that must be gone through. Some call it a "wilderness experience." Others might call it a "time of change." Whatever our impressions are, there is a period of confrontation between performance and promise. Mine came between a slip and a fall. Once you have an encounter with God through his son, Jesus Christ, you will never be the same! Never! Never! James 1:2 says, "Count it all joy"!

The will to survive is a challenge as we cling to hope. Peace, joy, and even love do not come easily. They are the outgrowth of conflicts and contention. Life is a struggle! The Bible demonstrates the battle of the rages. Life is the ultimate struggle of good and evil, life and death. The Christian walk is not smooth; there are many bumps in the road. Ask around, and you will hear that the testimonies of our faith are on the battlefield of sin. We fail to accept the responsibility that the struggle belongs to us. God is life! Jesus Christ is victorious over all!

Life takes root either by our immersion in our faith or our fear. Faith is a struggle. We must go through it to gain stimulation and strength. Truth clashes with lies. A choice has to be made. Change makes it happen. Change does not necessarily occur in others as much as it is developed in us. There is no conflict of interest; neither is there an exchange. It is an absorption. We can come to Jesus Christ with confession, but we must go through Jesus Christ—the crystal one—under the will of repentance to gain salvation.

Life journeys take many twists, turns, flips, and flops. To what are we to aspire? What is the position of our inspiration? Are we ever going to be free? Days come and nights fall. Airwaves escalate echoes of human sufferings. We talk about it, but never care to explain. Why the grip? The epic of times bears evidence that Jesus said, "If my people, which are called by my name, shall humble themselves, and pray, and seek my face, and turn from their wicked ways; then will I hear from heaven, and will forgive their sin, and will heal their land" (2 Chronicles 7:14). Somehow we must get back to basics. This is a new day! The reflections of our past have uncovered our identity. Past, present, and future, we belong to a loving, caring Father who will never let go. Hold tight to His "unchanging hands." Never let Him go.

Life is for living! The value of life has three components. First is comprehension. I was once told that understanding is the essence of life. To forgive, you must understand the situation. If we understand a problem, we do not give up so easily. Second is composition, which is a matter of life choices developed through admissions and acquisitions. It is what we allow to come into our lives, where we permit life to take us, and many times leave us. The third is completion, which is perfection. It is a continuation until we reach our true destiny—a holy life!

The trends in life have an on-time line effect. The "before and after" generate movement in unity, variation, and sequence. Unity keeps pace with togetherness. Variation flows with closeness. Now is the right time; there might not be a next time. We are coming near the outcome, and we will never turn back the time. Time and order pull after the leading strings of life to draw and connect. Time is, time was, time will ever be. This is our will in the pursuit of purpose. All time has intention, preparation, and completeness. What we do after the

45

storm passes over is just as important as how we go through the storm. The results make the difference. Time builds the premise of character to evaluate the purpose. An older woman told me a long time ago, "In a hundred years from now, I won't know the difference." Time outlives our problems.

Our praise will be to glorify His holy and righteous name in the sanctuary. No one will have to pump us up. Why? His word in us will illuminate the vision of His likeness so much that we will be the sanctuary, lit up and willing to be "like" God in spirit and in truth.

We want changes in our lives. We need changes in our world. Prayer is the essence of life. Light up your life with it. Pray to your children while they are young and have a willing heart and open ears. Pray for them as they grow and mature. Pray with them every chance you get.

My Grandmother Ida, small in stature (she weighed only 110 pounds), was the mother of eight children, including three sets of twins. Whenever we visited her, every Wednesday afternoon, all of us had to kneel down in a straight line in front of that beat-up, red velvet, hand-me-down couch, and our Reverend Turns prayed over us. I did not know then, but I know now why prayer was so vital in her life. Those prayers got me out of many dangerous snares in life, and Jesus opened a blind boy's eyes. They are teaching me how to cope (yes, even now) in a world I do not understand. Meekly and mildly, Grandma prayed. Even on her deathbed she prayed: "Lord, please do not let my children or my grandchildren go so far out into the world that they cannot find their way back to you."

Lost in the wilderness, wandering around, trying to find the way out is a dangerous place to be if you don't have survival skills. Our young people are searching desperately; unfortunately, we have lost our way. How can we show them what we do not care to know?

I thought I had it all together. I was in a spiritualistic church, but I was still lost. I was caught up in a windstorm, being tossed here, there, and everywhere until a grape led me into the wilderness of life. Being made into the likeness of God is the only thing that can satisfy a hungry soul, pierce through a raging heart, or calm the wiles of a fearful, anxious spirit. The great encounter takes place during the process through which we are made into His likeness. It is where the designer changes His design and makes it into His likeness. The likeness of God is the crown of life.

God is so wonderfully awesome! He takes the smallest thing in its simplest form to show us His greatest power. One day, this half-ripened grape lost her grip. As she was falling, she grabbed hold of the clinging vine. She clung to the word of God, because she knew from where it came. Her greatest desire is to be pruned and given back her fruit-bearing buds so she can go into the world and harvest souls for God's soon-coming kingdom!

The Great Preparation

Can't you see it? Can't you feel it?

The greatest preparation for the greatest manifestation

in the presence of our time!

Can't you see it? Can't you feel it?

The mass production of our children's

massive destruction:

Hope is shattered, faith is scattered, love is battered,

nothing seems to matter.

The structure of life forces our hope to decline.

Can't you see it? Can't you feel it?

The shift in nature, the focus of its display.

Can't you see it? Odd roses blooming

on a warm November day.

Time is running fast. Time is surely slipping away.

Morning is no longer morning before

night sways to another day.

Life is changing. The food doesn't taste the same.

49

We no longer bless it in Jesus's holy name.

Can't you see it? Can't you feel it?

Haven't you heard? Are you blind?

Jesus is coming! No delay! He is on His way!

He will be here in the prediction of His own time.

Can't you see it? Can't you feel it?

The vision is very clear. The climate is ever so near.

If you're in doubt, you will soon find out.

God's Kingdom is coming soon! This

message is nothing new.

Every word God promises is everlasting and true.

God's great Kingdom is coming to

earth, with or without me or you.

BETWEEN THE VINE

As we live, we grow. Growth is a mystery of unfolding miracles. Miracles do happen, and they are happening in today's world. Life within itself is a dynamic force of advancement. God did not stop His mighty works at the creation. He is still moving mountains and manifesting worlds upon worlds toward an end-time harvest. The reproduction of life exemplifies that growth is a mystery and a miracle. The seed of life is evidence of a right-now miracle!

The growth of a seed determines whether it lives or dies. The strength of the seed depends on the enrichment of the soil, the environment, and the daily care. Sometimes all of these factors are performed and yet the seed dies.

Remember, God provides the increase. We are the fruit of the divine vine. No vine! No juice! No Jesus! No joy!

During one of my hospitalizations, I was told that I needed a pacemaker. I was horrified! I could not fathom the notion. A long time before that day, I had made Jesus my CEO of the life God gave to me. I made a promise that, if I could not work it out, I would turn it over to Him! No matter what, I would not make a decision without His approval.

I was confronted with a major decision, which greatly depended on my heavenly Father's word: "Rejoice and be exceedingly glad" (Matthew 5:12). Also, "I am with you, saith the Lord" (Haggai 1:13). I got up, took my shower, prayed, and got back in the bed. I prayed every time I thought about the pacemaker. As I looked into the gloomy sky, I heard a still, small voice saying, "No." At that time, my daughter and the transport men entered the room. "Are you ready Frances?" During the ride to the operating room, they were joking and laughing, and I was thinking and praying.

Waiting is the most difficult part of prayer life. It is an own–up-to-it time (confession), a throw-it-off time (overcoming guilt), and a see-your-way-clear time (victory!). The growth between the vine is where we must struggle with conflict and conviction, to comfort a troubled mind. It is the suffering through pain that brings pleasure to desire. It is what we do and what we say that bring joy to the heart.

When we grow between the vine (Jesus), our spirit gets to know perfect freedom. There is a shift between transformation and conformation. It is where we feast upon the bread of life and drink from the fountain of living waters forever. Between the vine is protection. Believers are taken through the vine between the seen and unseen. *Growth is silent!*

Between the vine is where our spirit grows deeper, as we fellowship with Jesus. We are wedged between the vine clinging on for dear life as we are crushed into God' goodness, mercy, and love. Within the vine is the core and the sap. The sap rejuvenates the core and causes it to spring forth with goodness. Life experiences, good or bad, are active forces coming together to spring our growth and maturity into action. In exchange for our bitterness, resentment, rebellion, guilt, and pain, God gives us His goodness. I no longer live to listen "for" God's voice, I listen "to" God's voice, and I live to do God's will!

Between the vine, we grow in comfort, innocence, and nourishment, in a living pattern of change. As we change, Jesus is there! "Where the Spirit of the Lord is, there is liberty" (2 Corinthians 3:17). We have all sinned and come short of the glory of God. Jesus Christ changes Christians as well as sinners. He shifts our unrighteousness for His righteousness. Growth comes between passion and purpose. The primary source of growth is the pursuit of purpose. The impact of pain and suffering will influence the heart to act. The different stages of our life experiences present active forces coming together. Love is the most active force in life. Prayer is the motivator. Love and prayer activate the mind and heart to transform faith. *Growth comes through submission and surrender.*

In the operating room, a man in white secured my hands as he told me that my doctor was running a little late. As I was lying there looking up, I remembered the still, small voice. I said to the man in white, "Please untie me." The look of disbelief was in his face, so I repeated my request: "Please untie me." He said, "Here comes your doctor right now!" My doctor apologized for being late. I responded, "That's all right, Doctor, because I have decided not to have the procedure done." My doctor said, "Frances, I have explained to you that you need this procedure, and I'll say it again. You could be walking down the street or shopping in the grocery store and suddenly pass out." I said, "I know the risk, but my answer is no. Untie me, please." The doctor saw my determination, so he instructed the man in white to untie me and put me in the hallway. From the hallway, I went back to my room in complete calmness and joy. I felt peace beyond my understanding! Thank you, Lord! You allowed me to hear your still, soft voice! I pray for others that they will incline their ears to hear and their minds to obey. Amen.

When you are sick with complications, it seems that you are never going to get well. Waiting on the Lord to renew your strength can seem to take forever. Spiritual growth changes the mind to transmit and to transcend righteousness. For example, courage demands us to speak against evil acts. It takes times to expand and extend, strength to induce and endure, and fortitude to enlarge and magnify. As quiet as it is kept, growth is evidence of God's wonderful working power. It is an age-old process that is still going on every day we live, yet we are unaware of its presence. *We grow in silence between the vine of life.*

Maturity takes both time and strength. Waiting on the Lord can be a long-time process; however, it does not take forever, because we grow in silence between the vine of life. The wait may seem to last a lifetime, but it does not. God always provides an escape. He always answers prayer!

Time After Time

There is a time after time
between hope in sadness to comfort a troubled mind
There is a time after time
between healing in sickness the body seeks to find
There is a time after time
between love and hate, war and peace, bitter and sweet
There is a time after time
between clashes of struggle and the victory in defeat.

There is a time after time
between within and withhold to satisfy a life without
There is a time after time
between the measure of pleasure and the suffering in pain
There is a time after time

between what we say and what we say we will do

There is a time after time

between desires and dreams for what determination will gain.

There is a time after time

between prayer and praise, passion and purpose, and the will to pursue

There is a time after time

between the difficult times in darkness those rugged, rough, and tough times, a wilderness journey to survive, we all must travel, we all must go through

There is a time after time

between good and evil, growing, knowing, and showing a new life overview

There is a time after time

between reflection, realization, revelation to reason the reaction to renew.

There is a time after time

between enlightenment, encouragement, experience, and

encounter

There is a time after time

between situations we want to change, but there is nothing

about them we can do

There is a time after time

between performance and perfection when God's will

comes to view

There is a time after time

between disappointment, despair, disillusion, and

discouragement

between all time thank God once more in his time he

brought you through.

Symptoms cause pain
Good health you hope to gain.

Visualize the light from the cross
As God's love moves within every part of you.

Suddenly no more pain
Human tongue can never explain
God's powerful healing process
Performed in Jesus's name.

A DAY TO REMEMBER

The reality of life connects the past, present, and future. Remembrances connect the past to the present and impact the future. Recalling the past, we gain more knowledge of how to avoid present and future pitfalls. God is present and is an active force in every aspect of life! Life is the essence of being alive and well. The security and certainty of existence is the source of life, which comes from a living, caring, powerful God. He is the breath and bread of life! He is the living water! He is the resurrection! In God life lives forevermore. John 6:69 "And we believe and are sure that thou art that Christ, the Son of the living God."

We should live to love God. Living in love with God requires us to live holy, because God is holy. The Holy Spirit guides us into the requirements of holiness: "[1] to fear the

Lord thy God, [2] to walk in all his ways, and [3] to love him, and [4] to serve the Lord thy God with all thy heart and with all thy soul" (Deuteronomy 10:12-13). Additionally [5], we must "keep His charge, and his statutes" (Deuteronomy 11:1). Study and obey these instructions from Deuteronomy 10:12–13. The highest quality of duty is to love, show deep appreciation, and to be willing to serve and obey. Stay in prayer always. Let the Holy Spirit guide you!

"Remember the sabbath day, to keep it holy" (Exodus 20:8). The Sabbath day is profoundly unique. The Creator reminds the highest form of all his creation (us) never to forget about Him. This day was observed by our Lord and Savior, Jesus Christ. The Sabbath was made for man, and not man for the Sabbath. Therefore, the Son of Man is Lord of the Sabbath (Mark 6:2). The first day of the week is recognized by Christians (John 20:1). We should be eager to return to the reflections of our root, God's word, the Bible (Genesis 1:1). The Sabbath Day is one day out of seven, and must be kept to be in fellowship with our heavenly

Father—one day in seven to keep the memories alive, keep the memories close, and keep the memories holy.

Keep the memories alive: The power of a thought is amazing. It resides in the confinement of the mind. Ideas, pros or cons, and the notation of opposition occur in the seat of the mind. The ability to obtain authority is transcended though the power of a thought. Little thought means little effect, which brings little results. "Think before you speak," "say what you mean," and "watch and pray before you act" are expositions of a thought that typify the intent of action. The expansion of our hearts magnifies our soul to keep memories alive. Decorate your life with adoration, devotion, and aspiration for the great things God has done (Read Deuteronomy 7:9).

Keep the memories close: To make wise choices, the heart must be in the right position. It must be safeguarded always with mediation on God's word and goodness. Lock your memories in the chambers of your heart. Pray every chance your get. Prayer will keep you closer to God. His

Holy Spirit will protect, comfort, teach, and guide you. "Lord, empty out all my unwillingness and set me free— free so that I can be what you want me to be. Lord, fill me up as you." "Create in me a clean heart, O God; and renew a right spirit within me. Cast me not away from thy presence; and take not thy holy spirit from me. Restore unto me the joy of thy salvation; and uphold me with thy free spirit" (Psalm 51:10–12). Indeed, those who have experienced God's goodness have an obligation. "Then I will teach transgressor thy ways; and sinners shall be converted unto thee" (Psalm 51:13).

Good vision makes everything crystal clear. Images are vital to what really appears. The evidence of visibility depends greatly on the images we see. Without it, we go astray. As we look back we are reminded to "Keep thy heart with all diligence; for out of it are the issues of life" (Proverbs 4:23). Looking back in time beyond the draperies of distance and time, we are reminded to recapture, respect, and revisit our past. Keep the vision alive!

Looking back requires keeping up. Keeping up demands practice and exertion. To be redeemed from oblivion, our past must be traceable, trustworthy, and transferrable. In keeping up with our Christian heritage, we can say it is definable, conceivable, and believable, because it is livable. We have a tendency to forget, because we do not want to remember. God never forgets about us. When we woke up this morning he had already declared it a new day with new mercies and undeserved blessings. How can we not celebrate a wonderful God like Him?

Keep the memories Holy! Keep God's name holy! Looking back, we move forward. Come and go with me to my Father's house. It is in the fruitful valley of heavenly bliss where there is love, joy, and peace! The Sabbath is every day! True worship is celebrated in my Father's house, because there is nothing to desire, will, gain, or prove. The heart is filled with purity, passion, and praise ready to serve and obey. Come and go!

Love, honor, and obedience lead us into remembering God's goodness. The highest quality of love is exhibited through the spirit of appreciation and the willingness to obey. Never stop observing the mighty works of a loving, caring God. He is worthy! Remembrance is a continuation. "Oh that men would praise the Lord for his goodness, and for his wonderful works to the children of men!" (Psalm 107:8).

"For he satisfieth the longing soul, and filleth the hungry soul with goodness" (Psalm 107:9).

AN UNTITLED SONG

Every creature has a divine voice of direct communication.

Look at the birds. They do it so beautifully while perched

on a telephone wire or nesting in a treetop. They "cherup"

in complete harmony. We too have a song to sing! The

lifeline of divine communication is called prayer. Prayer

is an essential part of my life. I love talking to God! Let

me encourage you as my Grandma Ida encouraged us. She

would sing this song, which was written by Ry Cooder:

"Jesus is on the main line. Tell Him what you want." First

tell him how much you love him, and thank him for loving

you. Then tell him that you want—need—His Holy Spirit.

You need His guidance and wisdom in all you say and do.

Are you living in a roach-, bedbug-, rat-, and drug-infested

house or apartment where thieves rob you and molest your

children? "Jesus is on the main line. Tell Him what you want." Are your children and loved ones bound by sin? Ask Him to cover them with His blood. Watch them change as you pray! They will never be the same again! "Jesus is on the main line. Tell Him what you want." He already knows, but He wants you to tell him all about your troubles so that when your prayers are answered, you will know whom to glorify.

Prayer is the walk and talk of the believers. I love to pray. There is a place in prayer where there is sweet silence while life is put on pause. Prayer is an onward position of advancement saturated in an element of praise in complete trust with the expectation of confidence. We walk in the light, delighted in truth and trust in the spirit of Jesus Christ. "Humble yourselves in the sight of the Lord, and He shall lift you up" (James 4:10). In quietness and with patience, we wait. To avoid the entanglements, dangers, and hardships of this world, we must stop, watch, and pray. In times like these, we need a go between to give us hope to live and strength to gain the victory. We are wedged between good and evil as we seek our way back from the cross. After we drink from the bitter cup, we feast on the true vine of everlasting life. Jesus said, "I am the way, the truth, and the life: no man cometh unto the Father, but by me" (John 14:6). We must absorb all of his goodness before our vineyard can fully bloom. Eagerly we climb higher and grab hold tighter as we embrace the leading vine. Our new life in Jesus Christ is established in his love. He exchanges our bitterness for God's "goodness and mercy." All is renewed by the blood of the lamb! All is good! "Be fruitful in every good work, and increasing in the knowledge of God" (Colossians 1:10). Everything that God created was Good. Why not us?

It is amazing what our God has done for me during my recovery. With each pain, I became more alert to the way God wants me to live. I am like a grape hanging on the vine of life waiting to be used in God's vineyard. I am ripening more and more every day, and so will you!

Trust God! Have faith in God! I have been planted by the wayside of life. The storms of life have blown me off stony ground. Poor health conditions, financial discords, and other chaotic forces have tried to choke the life out of me. But, thanks be to God, they stumbled and fell. Every time the situation got almost to the point of being out of hand, I prayed to our heavenly Father, and he gave me the expected victory. The raging flames tried to scorch and stagnate my growth, but they could not get close enough.

Be patient in your prayer life. God said, "Be still, and know that I am God" (Psalm 46:10).

God has a remedy for every trial and temptation. Prayer is self-denial. Our reaction to prayer is acceptance or rejection. Disobedience brings destruction. Sickness is the destruction of life. James 5:13–15 gives us the remedy of how to deal with sickness: "Is any among you afflicted? Let him pray. Is any merry? Let him sing psalms. Is any sick among you? Let him call for the elders of the church; and

The Vine Is Mine

let them pray over him, anointing him with oil in the name of the Lord: And the prayer of faith shall save the sick, and the Lord shall raise him up; and if he has committed sins, they shall be forgiven him" (KJV).Through obedience we wait and pray.

It was the spring of 1985, long before my slip and fall. I worked for a national blood banking organization. I was the District Representative responsible for blood inventory for the hospitals in the Northeastern Region. Being the District Manager, I had to attend and present workshops. I held my position for fifteen years and loved every single second.

I knew that every time I set up a blood shipment, I was helping someone. I made many friends across the country. A high-level position always brings resentment. I prayed all the time. I know I worry God, but He does not mind. I loved the job He had given to me and I was going to make Him proud of me.

One day I was attending a meeting in Washington DC. I was asked a question about the activities of the district blood bank. I did not realize it was a setup. I told the truth, which pointed a finger at the District Coordinator. He gave me the "evil eye" that meant "Yes, I am going to get even with you."

After several attempts, his final blow worked out to his advantage. He had requested that the office be moved. The only way I could keep my job was to relocate. My husband was not in agreement.

I was asked if I would help with the relocation. I agreed. My family and friends were not so keen on the idea. "I would not let them use me," someone said. This job had been my lifeline for fifteen years, and I wanted to experience a good completion. I really did not mind. I didn't have another job in sight.

On my last day of work, the Executive Administrator came up to make the announcement formal. I decided to make us a lunch, since there were no good restaurants in the area. Besides, I loved to cook. He thanked me for my service and told me how sorry he was to have to do this part of his job. After he finished, I said, "Listen, I have fixed us a good lunch, so come let's eat." He was so upset he said he could not eat. "It's a two-hour ride back to Washington," I said, "and besides, I prepared the meal for us. Come on let's eat." Finally he accepted, and we had a nice visit. He was more upset than I. Later I learned that he had asked the building manager to look in on me. What that young man did not know was that, while he was telling me the bad news, I was experiencing a Holy Spirit moment. The Holy Spirit was telling me, "Don't worry. Everything is going to be all right!"

The next day a doctor came to the office and bought all the furniture. As he was leaving, he turned to me and asked, "What are you going to do? Do you have another job?" I told him I didn't. "How are your computer skills?" he asked. "I only have telex typing skills," I said. "You look very bright. You could teach yourself how to use the computer. Come to my office on Friday," he said, and he left the office. Thanks be to God, he hired me! May the good work I have done always speak for me. *God is good!*

RELEASED

Sickness disrupts the mere pleasure of living, as it inflicts

pain, suffering, and grief. Afflictions and illnesses damage

and demoralize physical and mental health. They block

the ability to advance, defeat our goals, and eradicate

our purpose. The state of being unwell thrives on stress,

concentrates on evil forces, and relinquishes faith. It is

a personal battlefield plagued with invisible forces of

evil destruction. First the body is abused, next the mind

is assaulted, and finally the soul is attacked. Sickness is

despised because good health—a promise of prosperity—

is unattainable. Every day I am cautioned: take your

medication, eat right, do not cut yourself, and be sure to

report any bruises to your doctor. Just like Paul, I feel a

thorn is in my flesh. I am therefore inclined to ask: What good is sickness?

Looking back to the day I slipped and fell, I am compelled to ask questions: There were so many people in that grocery store. Why did one grape fall from a bushel basket, roll into my pathway, and cause me to slip and fall? Why me? Why on a Sunday?

Here are some visions and conclusions from my ten-year review. They have greatly affected my life as a growing Christian. From the offset, let me clearly state: There is nothing good about being sick! Surely God, who is loving and caring, gets no pleasure from our sickness. He does not want us to be sick! Look at Jesus—there is no record of Him being sick!

A positive influence of sickness is that it reinforces the hope to gain recovery. Along with the sickness comes a ray of hope, and prayer requests for a speedy recovery. The endurance of pain results ultimately in the strength to recover. It is during the recovery time that God touches the body and imparts His strength for us to recover. Only God can heal and make life new! God requires our obedience and trust so that we can do what He has commanded us to do. Disobedience is an unattractive action hidden in our hearts, so deep that we cannot distinguish who God is. The world is infiltrated with lust, fornication, adultery, violence, using God's name in vain, and abusive acts toward others, especially our children. Alcohol, drugs, and sex should never have gained fame. When we speak evil, we seek evil. In our search, we become bitter and rebellious and eventually we become evildoers. Don't fight with Jesus. *He is not the enemy!* We have allowed the evil one to snatch away our willingness to live for Jesus. The world lies empty as we infest our lives with sin. Repentance is the willpower to turn from our wicked ways, never to return back to them. As long as sin exists there will be sickness. Reject sin! *We can do it!*

Sickness is never an action of God, but can be unto His glory! The recovery time releases God's blessings of goodness, mercy, and grace! Jesus said, in John 9, that neither the blind man nor his parent's sin had caused him to be blind. The man was blinded at birth. He was released from blindness into the sight of life to tell and show a blind world that only God can restore health.

The hands of the wicked have come against me. He tried to rob me of my good health, all my finances, and faith. Whenever the situation got to the almost point of no return, for His victory I prayed! The raging flames of his fiery darts could not come near me. At the name of Jesus, they stumbled and fell as He gave me the victory. We are released from sickness—all trials—with a purpose to demonstrate to others that what God has done for us, He will do the same for them. We do have an obligation: never slip back into what God has brought us out of.

Hurt, pain, disappointment, rejection, financial setbacks, setups, health issues, heartaches, and any demonic attacks come into our lives (and they will) at one time or another.

Rejoice! They are learning experiences to give us strength and power! Don't moan or groan! Put on a happy face and know that trouble is worthwhile, because when it is all over, God will be glorified. There is no room for doubt or fear when Jesus is near. Abide in Him. You are in good hands. Reach out and hold tight. Never let go! Great is your reward, if you faint not!

The fact remains that sickness can reoccur. Sickness brings us down to a level for changes. Sickness teaches discipline and submission. It is through the sickness of unforgiveness that we gain the confidence to forgive. Only a heart that has suffered in-depth misery, undergone hard, laborious pain, endured the pressure of affliction, struggled with a heavily loaded burden, can award forgiveness. Life demands the release of forgiveness through the will of a broken heart.

The sickness unto death is caused by the natural ills of old age and decay. The body rejects life, and the present time passes away. Sin releases its grip, and the hidden dangers of life are silent. The body has served its purpose. Life dies to sin in hopes of rising in hope in Jesus's arms forever!

Our first obligation is to our children. They have been deprived of the gospel of Jesus Christ. They are poor in spirit and broken in heart. They have been captured and blinded by our mess long enough. To resist their fall, we must openly introduce them to Jesus. For them to change, we must change.

The most significant characteristic of a vine is its capability to move. It climbs here and clings there to spread its grip wider—under, over, and around as it trails through thick and thin. A strong vine is firm and has deeply embedded roots. It will persist and resist any harmful entanglement of hazardous destruction. The vine endues chastisement, bears persecution, and maintains perseverance. It cannot easily be crushed, pressed down, uprooted, or stamped out. Yet, it cannot thrive without hands-on primary care. It requires pruning, pitching, and propping to prevent wild growth. All grapes must be picked in their season. Grapes, a fruit of the vine, if picked too early, are bitter and useless.

Life can be similar to the running wild grapevine. It crawls between the brittle thorns of disappointment. It is crushed by senseless directions of mixed emotions and confused minds. It is lost in the cradle of time. To survive, a vine clings to the protection of supporting elements. Our will to survive is hindered among the massive prickly briers of fear and defeat. We have not, because we ask not. Maybe we don't know what to ask for in life.

Grapes grow from within the vine one cluster at a time. In unity, they grow with each other.

An untamed grapevine can be unruly, if it is unstable. Its growth remains in limbo and is no use to the vineyard; it is thrown away. Unlike the untamed grapevine, we can always be used by God. His crushing time is our restoration time as he puts us back together again.

Between the fruit and the vine is the sap for easy mellowing and picking. If the grapes stay too long on the vine and become too ripe, they will fall down and rot. The world needs someone to fill in the gap to keep us from falling apart. Even with our best efforts, we have failed. The world needs a Savior more today than ever. Apparently we cannot do it alone. We need positive reinforcements to right our wrongful actions. We have gravely neglected our young people. We must offer them alterative behavioral attitudes. We must teach them, as the Holy Spirit teaches us, true love. Be patient and never comprise your faith in God. Don't straddle the line. They have a strong sense of what is right. They know the moment you step out of line. If the world ever needed a Savior, it is now. Introduce the children to Jesus! Just try Him! It is as easy as opening up your mouth and thanking Him from your heart. We have tried everything else. Oh magnify the Lord with me, and let us exalt his name together. (Just look over your life!) Great things he has done!

Oh come go with me as we cling to Jesus and save our children

Let us

Preach the gospel to the poor ... our children

Let us

Heal the brokenhearted ... our children

Let us

Proclaim liberty to the captive ... our children

Let us

Restore sight to the blind ... our children

Let us

Set at liberty those that are oppressed ... our children

Let us

Proclaim the acceptable year of the Lord.

Nothing happens without divine interaction. God is all wise and wonderful!

He is Alpha and Omega, and He is God Almighty in between!

He knows the ending from the beginning! His name is holy!

A LETTER FROM MY HEART TO ALL THE CHILDREN OF THE WORLD

Take a Good Look at Yourself

Come, my child. Sit down with me for a little while. Let's have a direct conversation straight from the heart. I am writing you this letter because these topics have a tendency to get out of hand, or at best they becomes one sided. Maybe you will give me permission to invade the privacy of your mind, as you gain entrance to these inner thoughts of mine. The punches are going to be hard. We are going to bump heads. There will be bruises, but no bloodshed. Never doubt that I love you, no matter what. We have drifted apart. I need this conversation, perhaps more than you. At least let me vent. Maybe, if you know the reasoning behind my actions, you will know and live up to your highest potential as you take responsibility for the choices in life.

The testing of our faith is on trial. We are stuck in a stale place. Together we have failed. Maybe by exchanging our thoughts, our minds and hearts will come clear again. Is your violence any less violent than mine? Violence is violence! It kills victims and promotes crime. Let's stop the madness and start to live again in Jesus's name. Stop living in the waves of destruction and the pathway of sin. Life is for living, not destruction that will end all.

I must admit, all your life I have given you what you wanted, thinking it would take the place for what you really needed. That was my biggest mistake. Now it is your time to give back. What have you to give? I allowed you to be the parent while I became the child as I relived my dreams in you to fulfill my empty life. Just like me, you refuse to listen. Just like me, you are shifting the blame. Blame is blame. Blame does hurt, but it helps us to straighten up and live right. If I have damaged your heart, well-being, and life, please forgive me.

Is your world any better than the one I left you? Will you leave to your children even a worse one? Look all around you. Gunshots ring rampant in the streets. Drugs still rule as king. Sex rates higher than the sky. Sorry will never wipe away our tears; neither will it bring back the victims of those precious lost years.

We all stumble, and many times we fall. Your life was given to me on loan. From the beginning, your life belonged to God. Life will seek, bend, crack wide open, and leave you to comprehend. How do you put things together? God is the only one who can put them back together again. You must confess the wrong and put blame where it belongs. Stop the curse. Don't let it go any further! Right always eradicates wrong. Right the wrong so that you will be strong. Remember, God is in every prayer, and He will answer when you call on him. Don't take my word. Try

Him for yourself. Always remember his promise: "When my father and my mother forsake me, then the Lord will take me up" (Psalm 27:10).

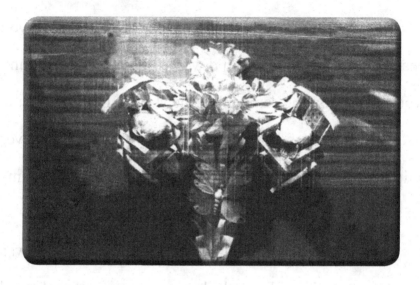

STEPPING OUT

When you experience an encounter with Jesus, you are inclined to do something better. As you rethink your life, you realize that the joy of the Lord is strength, serenity, and salvation. You have learned from your experience that "good and upright is the Lord" (Psalm 25:8). He is truly good all the time, and his goodness and mercy are available to all who are willing to accept it! This kind of truth is penetrated by the hard knocks in life. One must feel it to believe it. What makes a slip and fall worthwhile are the aftereffects. The determination that I slipped and fell once does not mean that I have to do it again. I got up in Jesus's name, and no devil can keep me from going on to the finish line. Yes, I am going to have more battles to conquer, more mountains to climb, and more rivers to cross. *That is life!* Going through this wilderness experience has reinvented my life. Paul called it "renewing the mind." Let me share with you eight ways to step out:

1. Approach every day and everything with compassion and thanksgiving.
2. Accept and appreciate flexibility. Try God's way! Read your Bible, and apply its teachings to your life.
3. Forgive your mistakes. Life is a learning experience.
4. Ask God for wisdom. Embrace peace and empower understanding.
5. Life is an open book. Focus and function on daily needs with daily prayer.
6. Inspire higher ideals, and encourage others to go with you.
7. "Remember the sabbath day, to keep it holy" (Exodus 20:8).

8. "Oh that men would praise the Lord for his goodness, and for his wonderful works to the children of men. Let them exalt him also in the congregation of the people, and praise him in the assembly of the elders" (Psalm 107:31–32).

Arise, My Child

Arise, my child, in the goodness of God! Take all your brothers, sisters, and the children with you. Do not leave anyone behind. Touch their lives with your rightful living. Let your life be visible and your vision be very clear. Get away from the grips of sin. Cry out in the darkness the precious name of Jesus. Don't be afraid, and don't be ashamed. You cannot fight sin alone. Jesus's name penetrates darkness. When you fall, as we all do in one way or another, guard yourself with His word and know His works. "Remember the sabbath day, to keep it holy" (Exodus 20:8). It is one day out of seven for reflecting on God's goodness, and getting closer to Him. One day out of seven to give God the honor, power, and glory that is due unto his glorious name. Arise! You must get up before you can stand.

Lord, I am keeping my eyes on you.

Be my vision. Be my guide. Be ever my life. To follow you, and to be ever in your presence is my greatest desire. To do your will is my constant hope. Lord, to be more and more like you is my lifetime prayer!